AF373968

TALES FROM THE HOLDING PLACE

GE Holladay

2024

This work is dedicated to my body
for carrying me when my mind could not.

before you begin...

I felt the call across the oceanic space.

There, once was home. There once was place and self and time and ground.

There, is now just just a dream. And one that concurs with nightmare whenever the mood strikes.

and the mood strikes twice daily, contrary to the myths of old.

The call came late. Late at night with my lover beside me. It came in the form of the softest idea, bled from the core of one come before.

The call bubbled up through my lips as I whispered aloud, "What if it's this? What if this is me?"

And my lover laughed and cried and took me to his calloused hands.

"It is most definitely you, and that which I love."

That call came swiftly and the dominoes have been crashing ever since. And while the oceanic space is somewhat neverending, I find myself in need of this curious magic to put my roots back in earth.

That's how I found myself here. In the Holding Space. A place of magic stillness and terrifying being.

Here existence is so powerful it chokes me. Here the softness of the air is so comforting it cuts to my heart.

I wish I knew the other side of it because then I'd be happy to stay here and make little campfires and light little thoughts into a thousand sparks.

Instead I soak in pain and I fester in healing.

Because that is the truth of The Holding Place. It is a sanctuary made of the things we hold tightly to. Where we can look at the walls around us and see our reflection in them. Where we can hold the traumatic baubles in our hands and look for a place to plant them.

Take a moment to be.

The Holding Place is waiting for you.

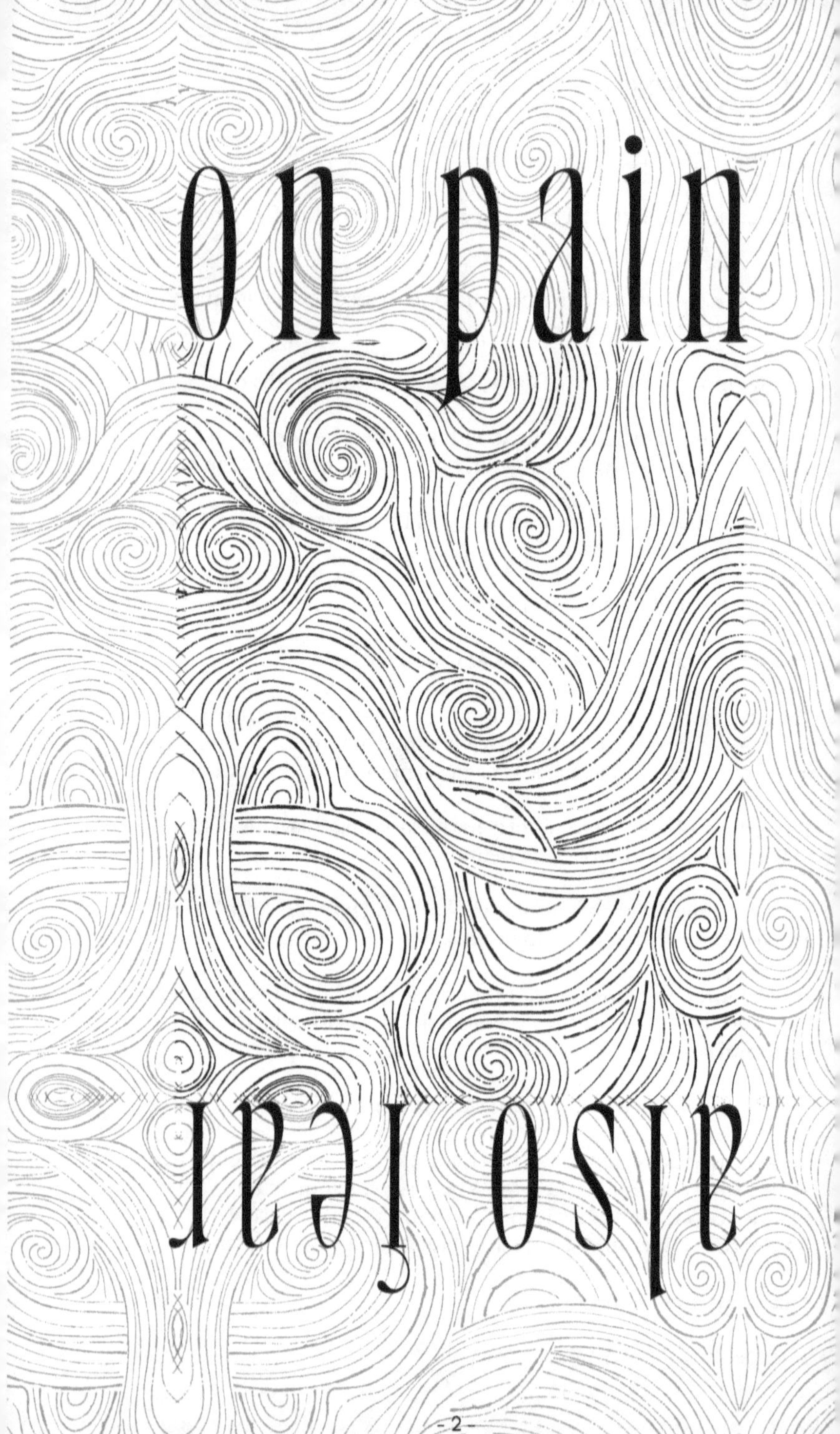
on pain

variations on fear

Think of
  fear.
   do
    not
     think of
      what can't be conceived.
       It is not
        fear
         . Is it
          not what can't be conceived
           ? I will not
            fear
             . I will look
              not
               upon
                what can't be conceived

millenialism: a reactionary tale

I looked around and blamed anyone not
currently enveloping me in a
warm and nonjudgmental embrace.

I blamed the ones I love most
because I held them to the highest standard
so shouldn't they be the first to recognize
something is wrong?

I welcomed new friendships
because they were a fresh set
of eyes and observations

...but couldn't get close to most of them
because they just didn't *know*.

pedestalled

It occurs to me that we were raised on pedestals; on a regular basis
we were reminded of our unique qualities;
the special that made us better. Just "better."

And no one said it was wrong; maybe it wasn't.

But I have to say, there was nothing to catch me when I
fell from the heights. There were no millions waiting to revere me.
There weren't even a few.

I was quite alone in my bloated mind. Surrounded by millions of
others who were alone in theirs.

And the worst part is...the ones I left, the ones that, like me,
scattered across the universe?
We all thought we'd have each other.

Actually that's not true, secretly we hoped it.
Outwardly we had planned to be gods.
We'd been told we would be gods.

Instead we cut ourselves away from each other...and we all lost sight of
any sense of God.

You see, our minds are so fragile; so delicately tickled with fancy and
intrigue; it takes a feather to change our minds...and while a thousand
waves can't break our will...our minds will break of their own volition.

Life is one giant tightrope.

We choose to walk it or not;

remain on one side

or another.

If we walk it, sometimes we fall;

to one side

or the other.

Time and experience make us all into excellent acrobats.

the right words

I get *excited* when I find the right words

cause it takes me so long to come to a point
when they come freely,

the rest of the time I'm drowning
in a sea of half-formed ideas and concepts,
all of them flowing down my throat,
blocking my air,
filling my lungs,
cutting off the connection --

-- to my brain.

It's ironic...
...cause it's my greatest fear...
...is that the right word?

You'd laugh if you saw me,
when the words come out
correctly,

I instantly fill with joy and my eyes go blurry,
I say the things,
say the words,

then eventually they stop,
because there's no more to say,

and you're just standing there
(laughing)
and suddenly it hurts,
(the way you're laughing)

because once the words are gone, there's nothing left,
there's only empty space,
relentlessly battered by laughter.

he says

Faith – faith my own.

Fear not what can't be conceived,

Will you follow, follow, follow?
Will you chase the world on feet?
Will all that I say become filth in your mind?
Will you sweep it away and forget it was there?
I have so many, many delights,

Take them,
uncover the mystery surrounding the blur.

castlesick

Do you ever miss your castle?
The turrets? The wind? The endless steps?

Do you ever get sick to your insides,
thinking of who's walking those halls now?

What jokes are they making at the expense of the cobblestones?
What ignorance are they spewing in the darker corners?

I miss my thirty-three bricks,
my hill-top home,
my singular tower,
my endless ruins.

I miss it all and it is nearly to the point of becoming nothing but a
fond dream.

I kick and scream myself awake from the thought that maybe
maybe
maybe

nobody cares.

nightmare

A new kind of nightmare;

where it begins in the familiar and strange of a dreamlike state;
nothing has consequences because your imagination can justify
anything...

but then reality *shifts*

and suddenly

the rules are the

same

as in the waking;

only the consequences from your earlier state of subconscious
are still in play.

Terror and panic set in.

I dreamt I was in an airport.
The familiar sights and smells.

Suddenly I was on the plane, and we were taking off;
the comforting pressure into the back of my seat;

and out my window I watched the ground drop away
and turn at a wild angle, but I wasn't worried;
my imagination told me there was a reason for all of this;

my eyelids were heavy and begging to close, so I let them;
and then pressure;
pressing me into my seat;
we were descending;

this is where my imagination went silent,
and the dream settled into a reality;

why did we lift off only to descend?
Did I sleep through the whole flight?

I seemed to be through the first leg of my journey;
then I looked for a boarding pass and found nothing;
I looked for luggage and found none;
I searched my memory for my most recent actions...and found a void.

I was pure panic and paranoia.
Some time later, I woke.

nothing happened

Nothing happened to me. Nothing bad or traumatic happened to me.
That's why I feel like a fraud. Nothing happened to me.

Not that I know of.

I honestly believe I'm the girl who called wolf; even when the wolf is
in the room with me.

If I say I'm not well,
Then I'm well again,
If I say I am well,
I am lying,
I am not well.
I'm well.

That's a lie.
Now I feel like a huge mistake.

Please don't think I'm sitting idly by,
No thoughts of how to overcome,
Just waiting for rescue,

No -- I am walking forward.
If I stop, I'll be eaten alive from the inside.

And I'm just so worried what you'll say if I start talking in the
meantime.

dear friend

Dear Friend,

Do you ever think of when we loved each other? Not at the same time of course. We passed right by each other. I think I even know, now, when it happened. There's proof in the emails. I tried to delete them all but there were so many -- and at the beginning they were so sweet and hopeful and delicate -- but also clumpy and sloppy and beautiful.

Do you ever think about me?

I know it's a cliche and I've tried cutting that cliche out of my brain, but it always grows back. I guess I just wonder what you do to handle it. Is it gone for you?

Are you free?

We skipped puppy love. I never had a crush on you. I broke the pattern you said had to be there. Maybe that's why I passed by your ship.

Why we missed.

Because in my head I knew there was no way it could happen.
Because you were shorter than me and I was huge.
Because you talked about girls you liked and I made jokes about everything about you.

I never had a crush on you, and I wish so much that I had.

You said the stages are attraction,
crush,
like,
really like,
and then love....or something very close to that.

And I skipped the first three steps. The strange thing is that all three steps followed eventually...they're still following me like lost, miserable, terrified kittens.

The regret I have when it comes to you is overwhelming.

But I can't find out what I did wrong. And I think you are more in love than you ever even considered with me.

I think you loved me very much...but I know you love her.

And she's yours.

And you're hers.

And I know that nobody is perfect; that, in general, all people are so capable of being absolute shits, given the microbe of a chance...

...but still it's the best thing in the world to be with another shitty person because then you don't want to be so shitty, and if you don't want to be so shitty it's because you found someone who doesn't make you *feel* shitty.

Thank God you have that. Thank god.

I need to get out of this place I'm stuck in.
The rut my mind is trapped in.
The ooze I keep producing.

I need to get out of it. And you lost your mind once, didn't you?

I only know some details because I clawed them out of our mutual friend. I still don't really understand what happened...but I'm beginning to, because apparently, I copy everything you do...at least when it comes to the mind.

I can't ever send you this.

I knew that when I started, I now know that in my bones.
Because I don't want to cause you pain.
I don't want to cause your soul mate pain either.

It isn't just that I don't want to cause anyone pain,
it's that that is the one thing I have decided I will not do.

I will not
cause anyone's pain,

not if I can help it.

And it's messed up and extreme and virtually impossible,

and that is what is killing me on the inside.

Because what's the alternative?
I could let myself fail and make bad choices
and then I feel the pain two-fold. In myself and for others.

Isn't it better for there to be less pain? Is the answer that I have to keep hacking away at life, leaving bloody stumps, and oozing flesh, and painful cries in my wake, all the while wiping the blood and tears from my own face?

I keep going and going and eventually it stops being the worst thing? Is THAT what it is to be fearless?

Fearlessly hurting myself and others.

No.

That doesn't make sense.
That's how psychopaths work.

I'm sorry friend. This has gone beyond you now. This isn't your pain to feel or hear or witness.

And yet it can't really go beyond you because you're in the way of a lot in my brain. I don't think about you constantly -- I really don't.

And I don't hurt every time I think of you....

It's just sometimes, like tonight, when I remind myself of who we were together -- that I miss you like I've never missed anything in my sad, weird, distance-ridden life.

Goodnight Friend,

S'okay.

on parenthood
also depression

when you were at my worst

When I was awake, not feeling brilliant or alive,

You with all your cheeks and cheery bliss personified.

Were I simply better, I told you, we could play

At the worst of my dead heart, you never stayed away.

My little long ridge lifting me with no strength but your own,

Worst of all is not so close and I, not so alone.

when i beheld our best

When have I ever been myself while you, more you, become?

I am not my own and so I make my guts undone.

Beheld the way that others say is best to birth and be,

Our little secret, you and I, is we need never heed.

Best of all I no longer fear death when we bleed.

piece and quiet

when you find a piece of peace in the midst of everything,
you find a minute of still,

a piece of your heart falls to the ground,
you pick it up and look at it closely, inspecting the frailty of the detail,
how the light passes through,

then carefully, so carefully, you fit it back in place,

and the moment is over,

the stillness breaks and you go on living.

there is no essay

You try and try and try,

then you mess up once

and THATS when you would have got what you wanted...

...IF YOU HAD TRIED!

Fail or fail not; there is no essay.

power

(You aren't powerful until you make a move
....but what if no one sees you move?)

You say you're so powerful,
I say you have to prove,

Cause where's your famous power,
If you never make a move?

my dad fell off his roof today

My dad fell off his roof today.
He lives on another continent.

I'm one week from being done with my current shitty job.
Still looking for the next one.

My roommate called today to say he has 24 hours
to decide if he wants to move to a new apartment next month.

My call.

I'm sitting alone at my favorite pub nursing a beer.
I don't even like beer that much
and I haven't tried all the pubs in town.

My sister didn't show up to the pub.

My bartender didn't even have the decency to be working tonight.

Fuck. This. Shit.

things that make me hate you - pt. 1

When you place amber amongst your other crystals
as if all it has to offer is energy,
and not a nation's entirety of tears and blood
encapsulated perfectly for the long ride on the black sea.

When you speak of Europe and all its many joyous cities
like Barcelona, Barcelona, Barcelona...
...but you've never even heard of The Land of Rain.

When you think snails are small creatures with flattish shells,
but they are actually quite large
and their shells are nearly spheres,
and they fill the ground like drunken fairies when the drops hit heavy.

things that make me hate you - pt. 2

When you laugh at the youth in my face
and cry out, "you've never seen a telephone!"

But mine was rotary.

When you dismiss your gaze upon mine as trivial
because I was born with electricity in my hand
But I remember abacuses in the grocery store.

When the world asks you to please calm down,
because it's already seen war and want and disaster before.

But you're not convinced anything else exists.

things that make me hate you - pt. 3

When you whisper my soul's name to another
in conspiratorial wonder,
unaware I stand so close.

When you are unable to see the beauty in the persons around you.

When you harm children.

childlike and motherly

Now I know the horror, it's hard not to see that former comedy,
blacker than the hearts of the men who wrote it:

The Common Housewife: An archetype.

A steryopipedream by the ones who were born but never bore.
The ones who were blood-got, but never Bleed.

I remember watching the dithering mothers of once before,
mocked for their strict sense of time and their stricter sense of what
must be.

I thought them funny,
these type-A moms with their schedules on schedules,
their lists upon lists,

their hearts on ice.

Now I know the truth,
it's tricky not to be sick,
to be honest of what I was taught by boys in men's clothing,
who learned it all from the Uptight Bitch Brigade.

You stupid little boys.

You make me *rage* and *cry* and *puke* at the sight of your mighty pens
scribbling nonsense ideas of what it was to be Woman, Mother...Me.

But when I look forward, *I see mothers who write.*

I see women who create.
I see He become She,
and She find their They,

and through our many painful transitions and detailed attentions
and obvious confusions
we fight and we free.
We plea and we change our sight.

Caught in it all with a sense of justice bought.

The price heavy: the cost of my childhood laughter.

on creativity

My Bad Friend, Sleep

The night for me has always been,
A storm to weather bravely,

And when that first reflected light,
Comes watercolor bathing,

the sill in blue,
that's when my storm,
has passed.

Thats when I know I am safe.

That's when I know that I have weathered it, braved it,
navigated and slayed the beast of starlight
...to make my way openly into
that watercolor morn'.

Now the flipping, now the flopping,
Now the search for endless pieces.

It falls to me to be the we that gives in to the paces.

So, sweet sleep, so long, feel ya later,
take me to the chances.
and when we meet again, I'll tell you
all the tales I've dance'd.

Children's voices.

Child cranes in constant hopping empathy within my brain.

Tick the tock,
there's coffee to be made.
Click the knock,
there's friendship to be played.

Living with the there that makes me fully in my melody.

secrets of

In this day and age, those of us wallowing in our thirties have a secret. It's our past. It wasn't all that long ago but we keep it shut tight and locked away.

Don't you feel that at times? Like you're a character in a novel. The mysterious newcomer who once led a life of espionage and intrigue, but now must pretend to be normal and not know any more than those around you.

But it all comes rushing back in dusty whirls of kodak memories when you see a photograph of some person who knew you in your former life. You can't remember their name, but the face is more familiar than you know thanks to the imprint made by your once infant mind and its once brand-new capabilities.

For a moment you consider the strange and friendly face...assuming, for a foolish second, that the person it belongs to must look exactly the same.

It's when your eyesight clears away the mist and cobwebs that you remember: that time is gone; that person is old, like you; that life is over. Go back to this new one...and keep your secrets secret.

the sum total of this bunting

The sum total of this bunting is as follows,

One part passion,
One part will,
One part obsession,
One part friendship,
One part friendship sunk,
One part joyous music on a ukulele,
One part you,
One part me,

Take these parts, string them up in:

JUST THE RIGHT PATTERN.

Display along the walls for maximum magical impact.
It's that simple.

And now, *increase the sum total.*

Until your home and your heart are strung up
with flittering, fluttering flags of soulbits.

Admire your work.

Thus ends the sum total of this bunting.

hammers on strings

When I play, I do not know that the sounds made
are coming from little padded hammers striking
taut strings that make a single, vibrating tone,

All I see are keys, struck by fingers.

My mind passes over information and looks to see
how many different keys my fingers can strike at once,
and in which order they should be struck,

My mind, eyes, hands look and listen for the complex combinations,

and I play them.

I cannot see the hammers on the strings,

I listen to how long the vibration continues,
as soon as it is over, time for a new note,

or perhaps there needs to be silence for a time,
but now I can go faster, faster,
and now another pause,

now I can make one, two, three, to three, two, one,
and now one/three, two/four, one/four, one/three/five,
one, two, one, two, one, two, one, two...two....two...one...two...

depending on how many a time is needed,
I cannot see the hammers on the strings,

that needs to sound more blue,

and that must sound more light brown,

more like sand,
more like flowers,
more like starry water,

These are not the names of the sounds,
of the keys,
of the notes,
they do not have names,
they only have meaning,
but even the meaning cannot be verbalized, in or out,

I see no hammers on strings.

realisticity

I,
can't,
see beyo–nd,

I hate using words like cannot,
only in its short form,

because it,
sounds,
so,
cheesy,

if only cheese was real,
then I could eat it,
for whenever I chat with a friend,

that I really,
want,
to talk to,

–

–

–
why do I refer,
to them like its?
That was silly,

it was silly,
now I'm in class,
like ninth grade,
when I was,

first,
introduced,
to free-writing,

because that IS what I am–
doing,

I am writing,

freely,

in here the now,
presently,
I am so tired,
sitting here,
sitting here is a cliché,
so why do I keep clichéing?
If... only....clichés were real...
and then....then I could get rid of them...

an actor practices her monologue

Violins, violins,
She paces, paces, paces,
Up and Down the low brick wall,

Woodwinds, woodwinds,
She glides–she glides–
Across the lake, green and rippled.

With a flourish she bows.

But
It cannot possibly
Be so easy

Like here, in the little kingdom on wheels; here there are all sorts
of people; sagging with sad bags of groceries; select plants spilling
from the arms of one small soldier; his face is smeared with jam
and sugary things so he is not well liked in this particular kingdom;
his mother stoops with the same as those surrounding her;
noticing the sullen stares all around, she swells with renewed
strength and resolve; stepping out, off, into the great world beyond
those sullen walls; bravely she ventures home to sweetly wipe the
face and arms of her little soldier; a kingdom to which she is
condemned every day.

King county compelled into countless moving kingdoms;

And one man is a knight errant...I know this because of the strong
steed he attaches to the front of our wheeled contraption of a
singular society. he climbs aboard and silently takes his seat.
Always with music playing in his ears...sometimes pages turning
between his fingers. He wears good shoes and trousers. The top of
his head is bare of hat or hair, but his brow is sharp as is the goatee
that frames his expressionless mouth. He always wears the same
worn jacket, no matter how cold it gets. It's in this that the best clue
can be found. Fraying, yet fiery and bold on the shoulder of this
jacket is a bright emblem of arms for a place thousands of miles
from here; is it a coincidence that this intrepid knight bares a
symbol dear to my heart for it's having raised me up in my
younger years? I don't know for sure...I haven't spoken with him;
nor have I heard him speak a single word aloud.

It's now that time of the night,
That my thoughts catch up with me,
The ones I kept delaying,
They turn up begging for a ride and how can I refuse them?

The trick is this: find reality fantastic...find fantasy to be real.

genius?

My genius will never be in me alone,
It comes in the combination of me and some I love,
And I love a million more than those who call forth inspiration,

Because not only those I understand,
Are capable of elevation,
I see how beautiful you are and you'll never belong to me,

You'll never know my name,
But I would -- I would give my life for you to be.

Just because.

a cup of coffee

Link my soul to *there*, to the middle of the coffee cup,

There in the crema depths, you see my reflection as it is: manic.

the worst year

This past year was awful. But I stand by my choices.

I decided to spend New Years in Jackson Mississippi.
I went to the theatre alone on v day and watched Pride and Prejudice
and Zombies.
I recommitted to bangs.
I took steps to be accountable to writing.
I left a toxic job.
I paid twice as much rent one month because I couldn't find a
roommate in time.
I started working three jobs again while in grad school.
I recognized that I may be suffering from either depression or anxiety
or possibly a nice little cocktail of both...
I recognized that I cannot afford to do anything about it.
I rewatched the office, Buffy, and HIMYM all the way
through...because, possible depression/anxiety/cocktail.
I became extremely financially dependent on my family for a good
period of time which may have spiraled my mind even further down.
I spent time with my sisters.
I designated a weekly phone call with my overseas parents.
I got a small tattoo that takes all of the above into account and also
honors the greatness of Star Wars; empire strikes back (there is no try)
I dressed up as Barb Holland for Halloween.
I voted. For the very first time.

This past year was awful. *But I stand by my choices.*

on healing

also love

me, a young girl, in reverse

I keep catching glimpses of her.
Brown hair -- simple eyes like squares with a tail.
She's got a quiet look about her. She is anything but quiet.

When she laughs, the world listens,
and when she speaks, the world laughs.

I've seen her pose for a photo like she's living en vogue,
and if I'm honest I'd believe it...shes just that captivating.

for a short time

I remember when,

for a very short time,

your circle ran through mine,

and we became friends.

numb

When my face was numb and I touched my face, I wondered what it
was that I was feeling.
It felt large,
bulbous, and warm.

It was my chin.

We think we know ourselves.
We think we know what we look like.
But we have to get used to looking at pictures and videos of
every angle of ourselves before we can say that we know what we look
like.

We think we know what we sound like.
But first we need to listen to our voice recorded over and over

And even then, we can't possibly know the extent of it...not until we
shed our vision and take on another's.

Did you know that you would be
A siren hanging over me?
Reminder of a gentler time
Harbinger of storm and shine?

I could never be like you
Always wise and always true
Navigating through the eye
Knowing well that all must die.

what we learned from helens and ces

Helens & Ces, the dynamic pair,

The greatest two in that cloudy nowhere since anyone else,
take your pick!

They struck their keyboards like the heroes they venerate,
They dealt a blow to my heart in ways I still crave,
They spoke of sex and sweat and sweetness....the sweetest.

Helens (I like to imagine) forges ahead with wings on her helmet: I see
her as a woman with many women within,

A kaleidescope of perspectives and memories and possibilities,

Yet somehow she is so incredibly grounded in her one-ness,
In her ability to pull from me the most tender of thoughts,
the most horrifying of realizations,

Somehow, Helens, you broke me again and again, and then smoothed
the cracked clay with new, vibrant possibilities.

Ces.

You minx. You electric rug. I don't know your face. I can't even
imagine it.

You were a helmet of pure technological art.

You wear a mask, and behind that mask, you protect the millions
seeking an identity.

Ces. You saucy deck. I love you greatly.

I learned a little secret that I have not told anyone,

At least not in words,

At least not to myself,

I learned a little secret that I love anyone,
Anyone,
It hasn't changed me,
It hasn't changed my life,
I love anyone; I could love anyone;

I will love anyone.

I am in love with sweet intimacy.
I am broken by sweet intimacy.

I have the sweetest memories of the words
spoken by Helens & Ces.

I remember late nights, reading and reading
into the depths of the world they borrowed,
And for a time, it seemed, it may never rest its head,

and I hoped it never would.

We learned how to love. We now know how to love.

he forgot

I'll always imagine the hurt on his face,
when I think of telling him goodbye and
not waiting to hear it back,
when I imagine not speaking with him
in a while,

but the truth is tragic,
there is no look on that face,
it's not that the love is absent,
it's just that he forgot.

blur

Even at our very best, there is only so much we can
focus on at once....if all our attention is taken up by the ugly,
the horrible truths, the terrifying chaos...it's plausible that
we have no more focus left for the good and beautiful;

which is equally true.

Do you ever feel like your whole life has been
some constant and consistent person saying:

"Well you could have avoided that...well you knew better....well you
should have tried harder...well you are responsible for that.
You *are* responsible for everything in your life."

I do.

Let the smiles go. Let them all go.

Release them to the wind where the breezy chariots can take them up,
Where the thundering hooves of intelligent emotion, released from a
thousand weeping hearts, can ride them far away where they will be
safe and hidden and unwanted by so many slobbering wolves.

Let the dreams go. Release them high.

Let the singular dream, inflated to an impossible size,
gently detangle itself from the rest, and soar above
to where no one can steal it, crush it, drain it, or worse...claim it never
existed.

blue bowl

My husband broke a bowl today.

I purchased it when I was 17:

Still very afraid
Still very worried I was not enough

Still sure I had a knight in shining armor somewhere out there
Still in love,

and yet not fully aware of how much love I have to offer,
and in how many beautiful ways,

I was 17 and we were in Italy,
Driving from one tiny town to the next,
Seeking out treasure like the pirates we were (back then),
Seeking out the most beautiful pottery,
for the most beautiful of prices,

And there, in a sun-filled warehouse,
brimming with clay and ceramic
and painted patterns of all kinds,

I saw my blue bowl.

It was by itself. It had no companion, no set, no family, no partner.
It was a terracotta bowl, painted sky blue on the inside.
It had the loveliest sprig of cherry blossoms painted on one inner side,
like a tattooed thigh.

I saw this lonely bowl and I saw myself:
No partner.
Soon to leave my familial set.
Already worried my pattern did not match anyone around me.

I saw myself alone and terrified,
and like orphaned Jane,
holding tight to a faceless poppet,

I clutched that bowl to my chest.
I carried it around for an hour,
unwilling to ask my mother if she would buy it for me,
because if she said no,
I might just crack...

She said yes.

I took the blue bowl across the ocean. It did not break.

I ate American cereal out of it; no physical sustenance to be found,
but savoring every bit of soul that was replenished as I sat alone
in my dorm room
and clung to this ceramic piece of my other self from before.

The bowl travelled with me to the other side of the dorm
where we had a view of the lake.

It travelled off-campus
to my first apartment
where I learned how hard it was to find 200 dollars for rent.

It did not break.

I wrote a song about porcelain and breaking and being afraid
and being so far away from anyone I love.

It did not break.

I took the bowl across the country to Seattle where it survived
five moves in four years.

It graced every kitchen shelf,
(or cardboard box),
or whatever else I was gifted in a home.

I took it back to Mississippi and by now I knew...it could not break.
By now I knew,
I was invincible.
Not to pain, not to hurt; but now I knew I would not break easily,

so I stopped worrying.

Then I had a partner:
While I was painted blue on the inside, he was painted turquoise.
While I had cherry blossoms, he had daisies.
While I was sure, he was not,

and we even switched places for a time.
We were two very different bowls that wanted
very badly
to sit on a shelf together,
(occasionally stacked one on top of the other -- heehee)

We moved. And then again. And then we drove two thousand miles,
filled to the brim with hope, fear, and stacks of ceramic dreams.

We made it to a little home. We unpacked.

The little blue bowl did not break.

My partner broke a bowl today

My partner, pregnant as he is with ideas, desires and emotions,
often lets go when the thing in his hand is breakable.

My husband, pregnant as he is, with fear, sadness and hurt,
so often does not see the hard cast iron of the sink
and how it will be unforgiving upon the glass in his hand.

My lover burns his fingers on the oven, baking bread.

My husband bears the scars of my words as I shout my fears at him.

My partner wears a long ribbon of scar on his forearm,
where he once flew late at night while the moon egged him on.

My lover is fearless and I am *full* of fear.

And while the world gifted one to him and the other to me,
I cannot help but hope that our two very different patterns
look similar from a distance.
I cannot help but hope that breaking is not the end.

My husband broke my blue bowl today. I was sad.

By the time I learned of this tragedy,
he had already glued the pieces back together and assured me
it would hold liquid.

I see only the crack.

I see only the extra chip off the rim.

I keep seeing him drop it in the sink where the unforgiving cast iron
of an older way of life splits this 17 year old me in half,
losing a tiny chip down the drain. What part of me was that?
I'll never know for sure, as I wasn't there when it happened.

He was there. He was there when my 17 year old self screamed out in
pain and confusion. I am angry that he broke it. I am angry that he is
not weeping with me. I am hurting at the sight of this forever-
changed object that still functions, but will never be the same.

That was yesterday.

Today, I realize that my sweet ceramic love
with his turquoise insides and his daisy decor;
my fellow object of hurt, desire, hopes, fears and otherwise;
my love who I sometimes dislike;

this person did not throw away the pieces.

He, having no idea just how hurt I would be by what occurred,
wasted no time in gluing the pieces together.
He didn't know that it wouldn't be enough.
I didn't know that I would still be sad to see the bowl forever changed.
He didn't know I had horcruxed a piece of myself into the object,
and now,
who knows?

He didn't know that I would rage and weep
and inhabit my own confusion.

He didn't know I would realize how very grateful I am that

this bowl is just a bowl.

I am who I am. I have not broken beyond repair.
I am not lost down the drain. I am still here.

I think I'm done trying to save the world

I think I'm done trying to save the world
Making myself messianic to move
mountains and hearts
I think I'm done thinking I am the one
The only
The best
The greatest
The martyr

I think I no longer need language to be my secret weapon,
feelings my public strength

I think I am done trying to save the world.

Because trying to save the world makes me lonely and sad,
Trying to save the world leaves me longing and heartbroken,

I thought my bloodless mission was this:

> *To teach an entire universe to be complex and creative*

> *To remind them of their (REDACTED)-given right*
> *to be amazing at absolutely everything.*

And if that were ever true, it's time for me to accept it too.

> That I can be good at stillness
> That I can be talented at silence

> That I can excel with my smallest thoughts, feelings, and tasks.

Its time to drink my drought of life,
warts and all,
and let the world take up the cry
against itself and for itself...and for me.

special thank you to the following folks for making projects like this
one possible:

Cody
Anthony
Ethan
Becky
Daniel
Marissa
Jacob
Kelly
Mikayla
Bethany
Aaron

It's love and support from community like you that gives me all the
hope in the world.

YOU are making the difference.